My New
Pet

Guinea Pig

Jinny Johnson

W
FRANKLIN WATTS
LONDON·SYDNEY

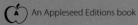
An Appleseed Editions book

First published in 2013 by Franklin Watts
338 Euston Road, London NW1 3BH

Franklin Watts Australia
Hachette Children's Books
Level 17/207 Kent St, Sydney, NSW 2000

© 2013 Appleseed Editions

Created by Appleseed Editions Ltd,
Well House, Friars Hill, Guestling,
East Sussex TN35 4ET

Designed by Guy Callaby
Edited by Mary-Jane Wilkins
Illustrations by Bill Donohoe

ISBN 978 1 4451 2201 4

Dewey Classification 636.9'3592

A CIP record for this book is available from
the British Library.

Photo acknowledgements

Contents

I'm very excited. My mum says I can have a pet guinea pig.

I want to know all about guinea pigs so I can look after my pet well.

Here's what I have found out.

Guinea pigs

are small and plump, with short legs and sharp teeth.

They are **rodents**, like mice and hamsters.

Pet guinea pigs usually live for four or five years, but they can live as long as **eight years**.

Wild guinea pigs live in South America. They often shelter in burrows.

Guinea pigs like **company**.

We've decided to have two so they won't get lonely.

I will look for guinea pigs that have bright eyes and a clean nose and mouth. That shows they are **healthy**.

A guinea pig's coat should be smooth and glossy, too.

Before we get my guinea pigs, my dad and I will buy everything they need.

We will buy a big **cage** and special **bedding** to put inside it.

The cage will have a plastic base and a wire top.

We will also buy some **food bowls** and a **water bottle**.

I'm going to enjoy making my new pets' home ready.

They can hide and sleep under here.

First I will line the cage with **newspaper**.

Then I will put in some **wood shavings** to soak up the guinea pigs' wee.

On top of that I will put lots of **hay**. They will like snuggling up in that.

I know that it's very important to keep my pets **clean**.

Guinea pigs like to be gently **brushed and combed** *to keep their coats clean.*

Every day I will take any dirty or wet hay out of the cage. Then I'll put in some fresh hay.

Every week I will take everything out of the cage and **wash** the cage well.

I will buy some guinea pig **food** in the pet shop. Every day I will give my pets food and **clean water**.

Guinea pigs like fresh food, too. I will give them treats such as celery, cucumber and carrots.

Some foods aren't good for guinea pigs. I will check with mum and dad before giving my pets a new food.

I know I have to be **gentle** with my new pets at first.

I might give my pets a tasty snack like a strawberry to show I'm their friend.

Everything will be strange to them and they might be **frightened**.

I will let them get used to their new home before I try to touch them.

Guinea pigs need some **exercise** outside their cage.

In summer we will put a **pen** in the garden so they can run around on the grass in safety.

In winter, I will let them out inside our house. I will watch them very carefully.

Hooray! I have my new guinea pigs.

They are both **female** and they are six weeks old.

I'm learning how to **hold** them very carefully with both hands so they feel safe.

My new pets
are going to be
very happy
and so
am I!

Notes for parents

Choosing a pet

Make sure you buy guinea pigs from a good pet shop or breeder. Take the animals to the vet for a health check. Ask the vet to check the sex of the animals too. Pet shops sometimes get it wrong!

Handling and caring for guinea pigs

Show children how to pick up and hold guinea pigs very carefully. Teach them to respect animals and always treat them gently.

Health

It's up to you as a parent to make sure any pet is looked after properly. Supervise feeding and handling, especially at first. Keep an eye on the animal's health. Check its teeth and claws regularly and take the pet to the vet if they get too long.

Words to remember

burrow

A hole in the ground where an animal lives.

mammal

An animal that feeds its young with its own milk. Cats, dogs, guinea pigs and people are all mammals.

rodents

A group of mammals that includes rats and mice, as well as guinea pigs, hamsters and gerbils.

mouse

Index